365 QUESTIONS
FOR TEENS

FUN, CREATIVE AND THOUGHT-PROVOKING
QUESTIONS

THIS JOURNAL
BELONGS TO

_____

_____

"IMAGINATION IS MORE IMPORTANT
THAN KNOWLEDGE."
- ALBERT EINSTEIN.

DAY 1-3

Describe yourself in 5 words or less

_____

_____

_____

_____

_____

In your opinion, what are the important things to living a great life?

_____

_____

_____

_____

Name 2 things you are grateful for in your life, and why?

_____

_____

_____

_____

DAY 4-6

What is one problem in our world that you think really needs
to be eradicated immediately? Why?

_____

_____

_____

_____

_____

What is your greatest accomplishment so far?

_____

_____

_____

_____

_____

Which fictional character do you relate to the most? What
are the similarities between you and them?

_____

_____

_____

_____

DAY 7-9

What lessons have you learnt from the mistakes you made in the past?

_____

_____

_____

_____

_____

How do you imagine yourself after 10 years from now?

_____

_____

_____

_____

How do you define perfection? do you think perfection is attainable?

_____

_____

_____

_____

What is the hardest thing you have ever done?

_____

_____

_____

_____

_____

Who are the people that you love the most in your lif ? What are their characteristics?

_____

_____

_____

_____

_____

Do you think adults praise kids too much or not enough?

_____

_____

_____

_____

_____

If you could spend a day with one of your ancestors, what are the questions you would ask them?

_____

_____

_____

_____

_____

Do you follow along with the news—either local, global, or cultural? Why or why not?

_____

_____

_____

_____

_____

What do you think when you see a homeless person?

_____

_____

_____

_____

_____

Do you believe in yourself?

_____

_____

_____

_____

_____

If you could change three things about the world, what would you change and why?

_____

_____

_____

_____

Do you save money? if no, do you think this will negatively
affect you in the future?

_____

_____

_____

_____

DAY 19-21

Write something short to your future self.

_____

_____

_____

_____

_____

What can you learn from your parents?

_____

_____

_____

_____

If you could choose, How tall would you like to be?

_____

_____

_____

_____

DAY 22-24

What's your funniest memory from your childhood?

_____

_____

_____

_____

_____

Are you currently trying to lose or gain weight right now?

_____

_____

_____

_____

Name 3 people you are grateful to have in your life?

_____

_____

_____

_____

Which famous person do you most admire? What makes them remarkable to you?

_____

_____

_____

_____

How hard is it to stand up for someone else? Is it easier or more difficult when people are watching?

_____

_____

_____

_____

Do teenagers today have it easier or harder than previous generations of teenagers did? Why?

_____

_____

_____

_____

DAY 28-30

In what ways do you think you might change over the next five years? Why?

_____

_____

_____

_____

What would your dream house look like?

_____

_____

_____

_____

What is one thing you hate about the school system?

_____

_____

_____

_____

Do you prefer socializing or being alone? Is there an exception?

_____

_____

_____

_____

What steps can you take today to better care for yourself?

_____

_____

_____

_____

What experience you've had in the past, changed the way the world?

_____

_____

_____

_____

DAY 34-36

What is one thing about you people don't often see?

_____

_____

_____

_____

_____

What is one thing your parents do now that you will never do when you have children?

_____

_____

_____

_____

How do you view selflessness? Do you think it's a good thing?

_____

_____

_____

_____

Make a list of all your dreams and goals?

_____

_____

_____

_____

How do you view marriage? Do you ever want
to get married?

_____

_____

_____

Do you believe being rich will make you happy(ier) in your life?

_____

_____

_____

_____

Write 5 things that make you smile

_____

_____

_____

_____

_____

Is respect ever inherently deserved, or does
it need to be earned? Why?

_____

_____

_____

_____

If you had the power to create a new holiday, what would it
be, and why?

_____

_____

_____

_____

What are you most afraid of?

_____

_____

_____

_____

Does your use of social media affect you positively
or negatively?

_____

_____

_____

Do you envy your rich or popular friends

_____

_____

_____

_____

How do you think your closest friends will describe you?

_____

_____

_____

_____

_____

What will you do today that will help you make progress toward your biggest goal?

_____

_____

_____

_____

If you could add, change or cancel the rule at home. What would it be?

_____

_____

_____

_____

If watching TV, social media and video games were banned today, how would you feel? How would this affect you?

_____

_____

_____

_____

What is your greatest strength?

_____

_____

_____

_____

Name one moment that you are truly proud of. Why are you so proud of it?

_____

_____

_____

_____

What steps can you take today to prevent other people's toxicity from affecting you?

_____

_____

_____

_____

What's your favorite movie? why do you love this movie So much?

_____

_____

_____

_____

What are 3 things that make you sad?

_____

_____

_____

_____

What lessons from video games do you think are relevant in real life?

_____

_____

_____

_____

What are your features that make you unique?

_____

_____

_____

_____

What do you think is your upmost responsibility?

_____

_____

_____

_____

DAY 58-60

If your younger self came to for advice, what 3 things would you tell him/her

_____

_____

_____

_____

What is your favorite book? Why do you love this book so much?

_____

_____

_____

_____

What is one thing you think adults get wrong about teenagers

_____

_____

_____

_____

Write about one thing you wish you had known 5 years ago

_____

_____

_____

_____

_____

How do you view attending college? Do you think college is Overrated?

_____

_____

_____

_____

Who are people you trust the most in your life?

_____

_____

_____

_____

DAY 64-66

Make a lists of good habits you desire to build?

_____

_____

_____

_____

_____

Which one would you choose: traveling the world or spending time with your family?

_____

_____

_____

_____

How much do you value your privacy?

_____

_____

_____

_____

DAY 67-69

What do you think people like most about you?

_____

_____

_____

_____

What do you like most about your body?

_____

_____

_____

_____

What are your biggest priorities in life?

_____

_____

_____

_____

If you were given 1 million dollars today, what would you use to do?

_____

_____

_____

_____

What are most afraid of about becoming independent?

_____

_____

_____

_____

What is your biggest weakness?

_____

_____

_____

_____

If you were given the power to invent a technology that could perform only one task, what task will you create it to do?

_____

_____

_____

_____

Are you who you thought you would be 5 years ago?

_____

_____

_____

_____

What do you like most about your best friend?

_____

_____

_____

_____

Have you ever fought against a bully? Why?

_____

_____

_____

_____

Do you believe true love exists?

_____

_____

_____

_____

Write 3 things that make your parents proud of you?

_____

_____

_____

_____

If you could change one thing about your life, what would you change? Why?

_____

_____

_____

_____

What city would you love to travel to in the future?

_____

_____

_____

_____

Do you believe in destiny?

_____

_____

_____

_____

DAY 82-84

What is your biggest regret so far?

_____

_____

_____

_____

To you prefer to be in the spotlight or
behind the scenes?

_____

_____

_____

_____

What is one thing you wish someone told you about
school 5 years ago?

_____

_____

_____

What are 5 things you would love to do before you turn 30?

_____

_____

_____

_____

If you could choose one superpower—what would it be?

_____

_____

_____

_____

What is most shameful thing you've ever done?

_____

_____

_____

_____

What does your perfect day look like?

_____
_____
_____
_____
_____

Have you ever witness racism? what did you do about it?

_____
_____
_____
_____

If you could meet one famous person who no longer
lives, who would it be?

_____
_____
_____

What is your most embarrassing memory?

_____

_____

_____

_____

What is the highest purchase you've ever made?

_____

_____

_____

_____

What is one place in the world you never want to go?

_____

_____

_____

_____

If you can only eat one food for the rest of the year, what would you eat?

_____

_____

_____

_____

Do you usually judge people by their looks (even though you try not to)?

_____

_____

_____

_____

If you could live in one place for the rest of your life, where would it be.

_____

_____

_____

What steps can you take today to improve your mental health?

_____

_____

_____

_____

If you can change one thing about your life, what would you change? Why?

_____

_____

_____

_____

Which do you prefer: video games or movies?

_____

_____

_____

_____

What does your dream life look?

_____

_____

_____

_____

_____

What new skill would you like to learn?

_____

_____

_____

_____

What genre of fiction do you love the most?

_____

_____

_____

_____

Are you afraid of leaving high school?

_____

_____

_____

_____

Write 3 things you can start doing to better
manage your time

_____

_____

_____

What do you like most about your favorite teacher?

_____

_____

_____

_____

If you could make one wish, what would it be?

_____

_____

_____

_____

Write 3 things you can start doing to better manage your time?

_____

_____

_____

What do you like most about your favorite teacher?

_____

_____

_____

What are some of the things you would like to improve about yourself?

_____

_____

_____

_____

If you had the power to change one thing about social media, what would it be?

_____

_____

_____

_____

Would you ever quit social media?

_____

_____

_____

_____

DAY 111-113

What do you think is the hardest part about
being a teenager

_____

_____

_____

_____

Do you read self help books? What do you think of them?

_____

_____

_____

_____

What is your favorite sport? Why?

_____

_____

_____

_____

What do you like most about being a teenager?

_____

_____

_____

_____

Do you think dating in high school is worth it?

_____

_____

_____

_____

If you change one thing about being a teenager, what would it be?

_____

_____

_____

What is the best advice you have ever received?

_____

_____

_____

_____

Are you an optimistic or pessimistic person?

_____

_____

_____

_____

What does growth mindset mean to you?

_____

_____

_____

_____

DAY 121-123

Write 3 of your biggest achievements

_____

_____

_____

_____

When was the last you helped someone overcome a big challenge?

_____

_____

_____

What characteristics make a good friend?

_____

_____

_____

DAY 124-126

Are you afraid of becoming independent one day?

_____

_____

_____

_____

Write 3 things you can start doing to help you
study more effectively?

_____

_____

_____

What does "work smart" mean to you?

_____

_____

_____

_____

DAY 127–129

Name 2 things most people don't know about you

_____

_____

_____

_____

What is one thing most believe that you don't

_____

_____

_____

_____

What bad habits would you like to stop doing?

_____

_____

_____

If you had to relive an entire year, what year would it be? why?

_____

_____

_____

What are some things you need to stop
wasting time on?

_____

_____

_____

Who are your favorite fictional characters?

_____

_____

_____

_____

DAY 133-135

How do you think life will be in the next 20 years?

_____

_____

_____

_____

Write down the names of people who are always there for you
when you are feeling low

_____

_____

_____

Why is it important to say no to people?

_____

_____

_____

If you could one movie or TV show, what would it be about?

_____

_____

_____

_____

What are some negative thoughts you need to stop saying to yourself?

_____

_____

_____

_____

Write 3 affirmations you would say to yourself anytime you had a negative thought

_____

_____

_____

_____

If you could travel back in time once, what year will you go to? why?

_____

_____

_____

_____

What characteristics do you think makes a good leader?

_____

_____

_____

_____

If you had the power to become one animal, what animal will you choose to be?

_____

_____

_____

If you had to live on an island for a year and could
Only bring three things with you, what would they be?

_____
_____
_____
_____

Do you consider yourself a leader?

_____
_____
_____
_____

Are you a morning or a night person?

_____
_____
_____

If you became president today, what's the first thing you would ban or allow?

_____

_____

_____

_____

What's your favorite song?

_____

_____

_____

_____

Would you like to be famous?

_____

_____

_____

DAY 148–150

Do people consider you to be talkative or quiet?

_____

_____

_____

_____

_____

What is your least favorite chore?

_____

_____

_____

_____

What is one thing no one will never believe about you?

_____

_____

_____

_____

If you change one rule in your school, what would it be?

_____

_____

_____

_____

What is your favorite subject in school?

_____

_____

_____

_____

Which do you think is more scary: the ocean or space?

_____

_____

_____

_____

What do you think are the characteristics that make a great teacher?

_____

_____

_____

_____

What does your dream field trip look like?

_____

_____

_____

_____

What do you like most about your room?

_____

_____

_____

_____

If you could master one language in one day, what language would it be?

_____

_____

_____

_____

What is the most important thing you learned in school NOT taught by a teacher?

_____

_____

_____

_____

What is one mind blowing fact you learnt recently?

_____

_____

_____

_____

What is your favorite memory you have of your friends?

_____

_____

_____

_____

_____

Do you often feel like life is redundant?

_____

_____

_____

_____

Who is someone who looks up to you?

_____

_____

_____

_____

DAY 163-165

What is one thing you've always wanted to do, but haven't?

_____

_____

_____

_____

Do you often worry about what others think of you?

_____

_____

_____

_____

What are you looking forward to the most about college?

_____

_____

_____

_____

Choose one: be an employee in a high paying job or
be a business owner who earns enough to live an average life

_____

_____

_____

_____

Do you have a favorite quote or mantra?

_____

_____

_____

_____

Who are your role models?

_____

_____

_____

_____

What's a career that doesn't exist (yet) that you think should?

_____

_____

_____

_____

Do you love meeting new people?

_____

_____

_____

_____

Describe your perfect meal.

_____

_____

_____

_____

DAY 172-174

What is the best gift you have ever received?

_____

_____

_____

_____

_____

What is one thing you think most teachers don't get about students?

_____

_____

_____

_____

_____

What is the best gift you've ever given?

_____

_____

_____

_____

_____

Do you think aliens exist?

_____

_____

_____

_____

_____

If you could read only one book for a year, which book will you choose?

_____

_____

_____

_____

Would you rather play a villain or a sero in a movie?

_____

_____

_____

_____

DAY 181-182

What do you think makes your generation unique?

_____

_____

_____

_____

Describe what a bad day for you look like?

_____

_____

_____

_____

Write a quote you would like to remember whenever you're having a bad day (in the future)

_____

_____

_____

What lessons from video games do you think are relevant in real life?

_____

_____

_____

_____

How do you respond to criticism?

_____

_____

_____

_____

What are somethings you can start doing to improve your self confidence

_____

_____

_____

_____

What is the best advice you've given to someone?

_____
_____
_____
_____

What movies will you recommend to your loved ones?

_____
_____
_____
_____

What are some things you can start doing to improve
your self-esteem?

_____
_____
_____
_____

Do you believe that high school is the best time of one's life?

_____

_____

_____

_____

Who are the people you desire to make proud in your life?

_____

_____

_____

What are some things you can start doing to decrease
how much you procrastinate?

_____

_____

_____

_____

DAY 192-194

How do you think your life would be if you were famous?

_____

_____

_____

_____

If you could travel to one planet, which planet will you go to?

_____

_____

_____

What is your favorite holiday? why?

_____

_____

_____

What is the strangest dream you've ever had?

_____

_____

_____

_____

Describe the oldest person you know?

_____

_____

_____

_____

Would you rather live in a cold, snowy place, or a hot and sunny place? Why?

_____

_____

_____

_____

If you could make one video game, what genre would it be in?
what would people be able to do in this game?

_____

_____

_____

_____

When was the last time someone made you feel inferior,
what did you do about it?

_____

_____

_____

_____

What is one thing you've leant from the recent pandemic?

_____

_____

_____

_____

DAY 201-203

What is something you parents often talk to you about that makes you feel uncomfortable?

_____

_____

_____

What is your favorite thing to do after school? Why?

_____

_____

_____

What is your favorite hobby?

_____

_____

_____

When was a time you felt betrayed? What did you say to the person who broke your trust

_____

_____

_____

_____

What's one trait you see in other people that you wish you had? what can you start doing to posses this trait?

_____

_____

_____

_____

How do you often respond to insults?

_____

_____

_____

_____

Do you often put pressure on yourself? If yes, how can you Start being more kind to yourself?

_____

_____

_____

_____

What are your parents core values?

_____

_____

_____

_____

Do you often find yourself over-thinking what you said or how you've acted?

_____

_____

_____

_____

What are your core values?

_____

_____

_____

_____

How often do you forgive yourself?

_____

_____

_____

_____

What are 3 things that trigger negative feelings in you?

_____

_____

_____

_____

What situations make you feel not good enough?

_____

_____

_____

_____

What self care exercise(s) do you practice?

_____

_____

_____

_____

Do you form obsessive or unhealthy attachments with people easily?

_____

_____

_____

_____

Describe the relationship you have with your parents?

_____

_____

_____

_____

Do you often enforce boundaries?

_____

_____

_____

_____

How do you perceive failure? Do you think it's important to fail

_____

_____

_____

_____

Where is your favorite place to hang out? What do you like about it?

_____

_____

_____

_____

_____

What kind of music do you like?

_____

_____

_____

_____

Would you rather date someone older or younger than you?

_____

_____

_____

_____

On a scale of 1 to 10, how strict are your parents?

_____

_____

_____

_____

_____

who's your favorite band or solo artist?

_____

_____

_____

_____

_____

what is the best school project you've made? why

_____

_____

_____

_____

_____

How do you handle stress?

_____

_____

_____

_____

_____

Are you ever rude on purpose? why does that happen?

_____

_____

_____

_____

_____

Which negative feeling do you avoid the most?

_____

_____

_____

What are some of your pet peeves about other people? Do you see these pet peeves in your own behavior?

_____

_____

_____

_____

How do you define laziness? Do you think it's okay to be lazy sometimes?

_____

_____

_____

_____

What genre of video games do you love the most?

_____

_____

_____

_____

Have you ever apologized to someone you have hurt? Why or why not?

_____

_____

_____

_____

_____

Which negative emotions are you most comfortable with?

_____

_____

_____

_____

_____

Do you hold myself to a higher standard than others? If so, why?

_____

_____

_____

_____

Is your inner voice kind or critical? What things does it say to you on a typical day?

_____

_____

_____

_____

_____

Are you easily influenced or swayed by the opinions and beliefs of others.

_____

_____

_____

_____

What does happiness mean to you?

_____

_____

_____

_____

How do you view procrastination? Do you think it's okay to procrastinate sometimes?

_____

_____

_____

_____

How do you handle negative emotions?

_____

_____

_____

_____

Would you ever quit video games and movies? Why or why not?

_____

_____

_____

_____

What do you think makes someone a good person?

_____

_____

_____

_____

_____

How do you define motivation? Do you think it's okay to rely on motivation

_____

_____

_____

_____

Do you think sports should be a big part of high school?

_____

_____

_____

_____

What do you hate the most about being a teenager?

_____

_____

_____

_____

_____

What activity makes you feel competent?

_____

_____

_____

_____

Have you ever deeply hated someone? Are you still holding that feeling and why?

_____

_____

_____

_____

Have you ever sacrificed a part of yourself to fit in with others better?

_____

_____

_____

_____

_____

What is one childhood memory that sticks with you. Why do you think you remember it so clearly?

_____

_____

_____

_____

_____

How do I show up for others more?

_____

_____

_____

_____

_____

Is it ever right to do the wrong thing? Is it ever wrong to do the right thing?

_____

_____

_____

_____

_____

How would you describe 'freedom' in your own words?

_____

_____

_____

_____

What gets you excited about life?

_____

_____

_____

_____

Would you break the law to save a loved one?

_____

_____

_____

_____

Do you think crying is a sign of weakness or strength?

_____

_____

_____

_____

What's the most sensible thing you've ever heard someone say?

_____

_____

_____

_____

DAY 257-259

What do you wish you spent more time doing three years ago?

_____

_____

_____

_____

_____

What would you do differently if you knew nobody would judge you?

_____

_____

_____

_____

What do we all have in common besides our genes that makes us human?

_____

_____

_____

_____

DAY 260-262

Do you ask enough questions or do you settle for what you know?

_____

_____

_____

_____

_____

If you could choose one book as a mandatory read for all high school students, which book would you choose?

_____

_____

_____

_____

What do you think is the difference between living and existing?

_____

_____

_____

_____

On a scale of 1-10, how happy are you today?

_____

_____

_____

_____

What's something you know you do differently than most people?

_____

_____

_____

_____

What is the most desirable trait another person can possess?

_____

_____

_____

_____

If the average human lifespan was 40 years, how would you live your life differently?

_____

_____

_____

_____

Would you rather be a worried genius or a joyful dullard?

_____

_____

_____

_____

What do you think is the difference between innocence and ignorance?

_____

_____

_____

_____

If you could instill one piece of advice in a newborn baby's mind,
what advice would yougive?

_____

_____

_____

_____

Would you rather lose all of your old memories or never be able to make new ones?

_____

_____

_____

_____

What's the one thing you'd like others to remember about you?

_____

_____

_____

_____

Is it more important to love or be loved?

_____

_____

_____

_____

Are you more worried about doing things right, or doing the right things?

_____

_____

_____

_____

Why do we think of others the most when they're gone?

_____

_____

_____

_____

When you think of 'home,' what, specifically, do you think of?

_____

_____

_____

_____

_____

What can money not buy?

_____

_____

_____

_____

What does 'peace' mean to you?

_____

_____

_____

_____

What is the weirdest thing some one has said to you?

_____

_____

_____

_____

What's the difference between settling for things and accepting the way things are?

_____

_____

_____

_____

What is your most prized possession?

_____

_____

_____

_____

If you could live forever, would you want to? Why?

_____

_____

_____

_____

_____

What good do you think comes from suffering?

_____

_____

_____

_____

What worries you about the future?

_____

_____

_____

_____

DAY 285–286

What is something you think is worth waiting for?

_____

_____

_____

_____

_____

Would you rather be attractive and dumb or be intelligent and ugly?

_____

_____

_____

What's the biggest lie you once believed was true?

_____

_____

_____

_____

What is the greatest peer pressure you've ever felt?

_____

_____

_____

_____

_____

What is one question you wish you knew the answer to?

_____

_____

_____

_____

What will you never do?

_____

_____

_____

_____

Do you sometimes deliberately try to impress others

_____

_____

_____

_____

_____

What chances do you wish you had taken?

_____

_____

_____

_____

What will you never give up on?

_____

_____

_____

_____

What motivates you to go to study?

_____

_____

_____

_____

What do you think about when you lie awake in bed?

_____

_____

_____

_____

What do you want less of in your life?

_____

_____

_____

_____

What do you want more of in your life?

_____

_____

_____

_____

_____

When you meet someone for the very first time what do you want them to think about you?

_____

_____

_____

_____

What's something new you recently learned about yourself?

_____

_____

_____

_____

Are you more like your mom or your dad? In what way?

_____

_____

_____

_____

How would an extra $100 a month change your life?

_____

_____

_____

_____

What things in life do you think should be free (even though they aren't)

_____

_____

_____

_____

What is something that confuses you?

_____

_____

_____

_____

What have you lost interest in recently?

_____

_____

_____

_____

What job would you never do no matter how much it paid?

_____

_____

_____

who do you turn to when you need good advice?

_____

_____

_____

_____

_____

What is something society can do without?

_____

_____

_____

_____

What do you think makes someone a hero?

_____

_____

_____

_____

What's one downside of the modern dayworld?

_____

_____

_____

_____

When was the last time you felt lucky?

_____

_____

_____

_____

What simple fact do you wish more people understood?

_____

_____

_____

_____

What are some recent compliments you've received?

_____

_____

_____

_____

_____

How much money per month do you think is enough for you to live comfortably?

_____

_____

_____

_____

What is your favorite smell?

_____

_____

_____

_____

How many hours a week do you think you spend online?

_____

_____

_____

_____

How many hours of television do you watch in a week?

_____

_____

_____

_____

Who is the strongest person you know? Why?

_____

_____

_____

_____

DAY 317-319

How will today matter in five years from now?

_____

_____

_____

_____

_____

_____

What makes someone attractive to you?

_____

_____

_____

_____

Why is it important to never give up?

_____

_____

_____

_____

What do you owe yourself?

_____

_____

_____

_____

How do you define passion?

_____

_____

_____

_____

What makes everyone smile?

_____

_____

_____

_____

What would a world populated by clones of you be like?

_____
_____
_____
_____
_____

What weird food combinations do you really enjoy?

_____
_____
_____
_____

What's the most expensive thing you've broken?

_____
_____
_____
_____

When was a time you felt betrayed? What did you say to the person

_____

_____

_____

_____

_____

What's one trait you see in other people that you wish you had? what can you start doing to posses this trait?

_____

_____

_____

_____

What is the most expensive thing you've eaten?

_____

_____

_____

_____

_____

What was cool when you were young but isn't cool now?

_____

_____

_____

_____

_____

What mythical creature do you wish actually existed?

_____

_____

_____

_____

_____

What's the most interesting building you've ever seen?

_____

_____

_____

_____

_____

What invention doesn't get a lot of love, but has greatly improved the world?

_____

_____

_____

_____

_____

What's the craziest conversation you've overheard?

_____

_____

_____

_____

What goal do you think humanity is not focused enough on achieving?

_____

_____

_____

_____

What situations make you feel not good enough?

_____

_____

_____

_____

What self care exercise(s) do you practice?

_____

_____

_____

_____

Do you form obsessive or unhealthy attachments with people easily?

_____

_____

_____

_____

How comfortable are you speaking in front of large groups of people?

_____

_____

_____

_____

_____

What's something that all your friends don't agree on?

_____

_____

_____

_____

_____

What's the most ridiculous thing you have bought?

_____

_____

_____

_____

_____

What habit do you have now that you wish you started much earlier?

_____

_____

_____

_____

What's the worst hairstyle you've ever had?

_____

_____

_____

_____

What's the most pleasant sounding accent?

_____

_____

_____

_____

DAY 343–345

What qualities do all your friends have in common?

_____

_____

_____

_____

What do you think could be done to improve social media?

_____

_____

_____

_____

Do you have a secret talent?

_____

_____

_____

_____

What's something that everyone knows is true, but we don't like to admit it?

_____

_____

_____

_____

_____

What's the best lesson you've learned from a work of fiction?

_____

_____

_____

_____

_____

What things are rarely taught in school but extremely useful?

_____

_____

_____

_____

What's the funniest thing you've done absent-minded?

_____

_____

_____

_____

What really needs to be modernized?

_____

_____

_____

_____

What was the last song you sang along to?

_____

_____

_____

_____

Which of your bad habits will be the hardest to quit?

_____

_____

_____

_____

_____

When was the last time you stayed up through the entire night?

_____

_____

_____

_____

What's the oldest thing you own?

_____

_____

_____

_____

Who is the most creative person you know?

_____

_____

_____

_____

What near future predictions do you have?

_____

_____

_____

_____

What profession doesn't get enough credit or respect?

_____

_____

_____

_____

How much do you plan / prepare for the future?

_____

_____

_____

_____

Why is it important to always be yourself?

_____

_____

_____

_____

Describe your relationship with your parents in 3 words

_____

_____

_____

_____

How would you describe your future in three words?

_____

_____

_____

_____

What's the most amazing place in nature you've been ?

_____

_____

_____

_____

What is the clumsiet thing you've done?

_____

_____

_____

_____

DAY 363-365

What do you plan to do after high school? Why do you want to take this path?

_____

_____

_____

_____

_____

What's your favorite question in this journal?

_____

_____

_____

_____

Did you enjoy this journal?

_____

_____

_____

_____

Made in the USA
Las Vegas, NV
29 December 2024

15526537R00070